BECAUSE WHEN GOD IS TOO BUSY

HAÏTI,
me &
THE WORLD

BECAUSE WHEN GOD IS TOO BUSY

HAÏTI, me & THE WORLD

Gina Athena Ulysse

WESLEYAN UNIVERSITY PRESS

MIDDLETOWN, CONNECTICUT

Wesleyan Poetry

Wesleyan University Press
Middletown, CT 06459
www.wesleyan.edu/wespress
2017 © Gina Athena Ulysse
Manufactured in the United States of America

Paperback ISBN: 978-0-8195-7735-1
Ebook ISBN: 978-0-8195-7736-8

Library of Congress Cataloging-in-Publication Data is available upon request

5 4 3 2

I can say that surrealism has historically responded to the necessity of conciliating [the] human condition in its both material and spiritual aspects. We would always reject the dissociation of those aspects from each other.

Andre Breton, 1946

There was dirt. Heaping piles rested alongside rectangular holes deeply dug into the ground in a faraway room adjacent to a temple with a long entryway barricaded with overlapping rows of barbed wire and cacti. We had come from the city

When I was young, I took part in a ritual that I can barely recall. I was never meant to speak of it. Part of its protective potency was in the silence that shrouded a too sickly, gangly body too often under siege.

Decades later, I participated in a reinvention of this ritual with a new priest in a different town. I didn't need healing. He wanted me there in the room so I could observe and learn. I was much older, healthier, an anthropologist.

It took a while for me to sew the handmade cotton vest. Did I have one all those years ago? Red on one side and black on the other. Thick strips of white juxtaposed over each other to make slightly crooked crosses. I did not have to pay, but he had specific directives:

You need to do the digging. Learn other languages. Do more research. Read. Keep doing the work that will take you back to see where this will lead you. No one likes to speak of this. Just keep reading and then tell *them* everything.

According to an old tale, *A woman who had become barren came to Judas the Pious for counsel; the mystic should succeed where medicine was powerless! He told her that nothing would help except that she be forgotten like a corpse moldering in the earth. To carry out his prescription he had her children place her in a grave; and then armed men, hired for this purpose, make a sudden attack upon them so that they were frightened and ran away, completely forgetting their mother. She arose of the grave, newborn, and in short order proved the efficacy of the remedy. The symbolic internment and rebirth freed her from the misfortune that was her lot in what had now become her previous existence.*

I grew up under a dictatorship. I have a complicated relationship with silence.

Sleeping Temple

Peristil an Dòmi

l'ap kraze
pa kite li kraze pitit
pa kite li tonbe
ranje li epi kite peristil la dòmi

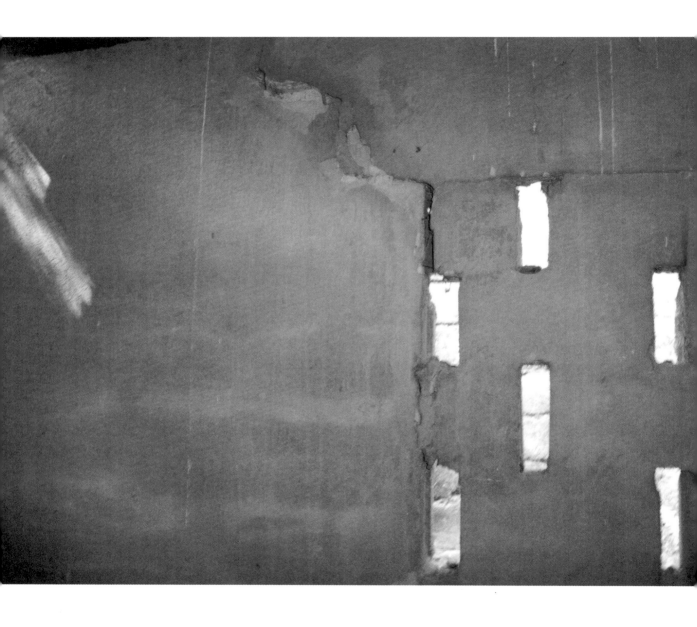

Peristil an Dòmi
(Sleeping Temple)

l'ap kraze
pa kite li kraze pitit
pa kite li tonbe
ranje li epi kite peristil la dòmi

(It's breaking down
don't let it break child
don't let it fall
fix it and let the temple sleep)

Because When God
Is Too Busy

The Hair Poem
"When are you going to go natural, girlfriend?"

Dreads
to her
they were the essence of being cool
the essence of being black
the essence of being woman
to her they were the essence of being a cool blakk woman
                                        Revolutionary Commodity
what exactly constitutes one's blackness
i've always wanted to ask
a black woman struggling
to carve out herself, myself, a sense of self, a me
with straightened, permed, colonized hair
what exactly constitutes one's blackness
i want to ask
i want to know
because to them i'm not black
i'm never really blakk enough
she
she   always
twirls   her locks
her   long locks
her essence of being cool
her essence of being blakk
her essence of being woman
her essence of being a cool blakk woman
                                        Right-e-o-u-s-s-s!!!

Concepts Of Home

I just left   it
lying   there   on the table at Espresso Café
a cup lined with fizzzzlessss foam
pressing the pages down
pressing to keep them down
to keep them closed
so Grandmere doesn't see them
if my grandmother ever read these words
echoing screams of Kundera's post-mid-life crisis
she would have raised her eyebrows
lowered her head rolled her eyes
stuped   real   loud
and with swaying hips of her womanly form
she would have walked away
with a bad taste in her mouth
                              that's my critique of immortality

I remember knees rubbing
as I tried to outrun
Katia who was always the fastest
she was even faster than Djeanane who was taller than all of us
blue/white checked pleated skirt twirls when I spin
          flies when I jump
          trying to reach extended branches
that were closer to the sky than they were to my head
I remember us collecting rocks
that I held onto tightly within closed fists
I remember running on paved sidewalks
                              passing the Cabane Choucoune
                              Le Petit Chaperon Rouge

on our way home we would stop at *a pye zanmann*
look for the   yellowish orange ones   the ripe ones
we'd throw rocks like boys at the *zanmann*
until we knocked them onto the ground
we would wipe them off our uniforms
and stuff them into our mouths
biting away flesh that was barely ripe for eating
but soft enough to let spots of juice seep through
leaving tongues tasting of sour
we weren't suppose to *keyi zanmann* on that street
or on any street

where we would be seen acting like *ti moun san fanmi*
ti moun san manman
my mother never knew we did that
unless
we bit into one so green
we had to spit it out quickly
carelessly
letting it stain our clothes

                                                    when I was in Jamaica this summer

I ate breadfruit and saltfish
I ate *bonbonsiro*
I cooked like Mother or Ivela would
I never measure anything
I cook like that
because that's just the way us women
at Rue Darguin No. 8 cooked

                                          at Dragon's Bay Villa
I skipped about in my yellow flowered dress
the blue bay
the escovitched fish
small strips of *kann* in a plastic bag tied with a twist
for the tourist price of 30 J
the smell of and the taste of blue mountain coffee
with carnation evaporated milk
to which I'd add spoonfuls of brown sugar
brown sugar that I'd have to demand
because raw sugar has no place on tables in hotels
it is colored
raw sugar has no place on tables in hotels
it is colored
because it is not refined
it wasn't processed in britain or in the united states
lean dark waiters in white shirts and red vests serving
uptight white american tourists who want eggs over easy
instead of ackee and saltfish for breakfast
who sit under the almond tree
my almond tree by the bar
drinking rum punches
the almond tree overlooking the bay
the almond tree I wanted to climb
I jumped trying to catch extended branches
                    jumped again
my dress
rode up
glimpses of the
eternal   thigh

                    up
again
I lost my balance
I lost my shame
as I jumped up again over and over again
trying to grab arching branches with almonds
that have not seen me for fifteen years
I didn't even check
to see if they were yellowish gold or even close
that wasn't the point
no
I had to knock them down from the tree
wipe them off on my dress
and sink my teeth into them
as soon as I possessed them
as soon as I had them in my hand
without wasting a moment
but they fell on the sand
I didn't even wipe them
I bit right into them
one at a time
because I had to
I had to because
they reminded me of the place where I came from
this place   a country   my country   a man
the *zanmann* reminded me of this man
this man with whom I shared a torrid love
a man who didn't like women
a man who smothered children before they were born
because in their mother's belly they promised
they'd have too much fire in their souls
they were black
he knew they'd all be blakk
he knew they were all blakk
and they promised they'd want to be free
and they promised they'd fight to stay free
because they were blakk
and he knew they knew what would happen
and he knew they knew what would happen   what always happens
he knew they knew they couldn't be french
because they only speak Kreyòl
he knew they knew they couldn't be french
pase se moun andeyò yo ye
the *zanmann* reminded me of this man
that I haven't gone back to
that I can't go back to
                    that I don't want to go back to   yet

that I don't want to see so   t o r n
bleeding
because I don't want to believe that ayiti   can
bleed
that   ayiti   is   bleeding
        I don't want to   see
                        I don't want   to see
her
bleed
ing
but it's always been—
he said
high
        suicide
                alcohol   ism
family
                                                    violence
        rapesrepeatedrapesofbabieschildrengirlswomenladiesgirlswomenviolenceagainstwomen
blood   has   been
shedding   in
                South   Africa
                                        black   blood
colored   blood
                        blood
a lot   of   PNP and JLP   blood

red   has   always   been   the   color   of   the   blood   that   has
                        c o l o u r e d
South   Africa

        how do you call a place home that doesn't allow you to forget
        how do you call a place home that tears you inside out
that makes you wish you could not feel
that makes you wish you could not think
that makes you wish you could not see
that makes you wish you could not remember
horror that has become an everyday commodity
a place that keeps bleeding
that keeps bleeding
even after operation restore democracy
that will continue
to bleed
until
                        until there's no trenchtown
                        until there's no lost city no sun city
                        until there's no white power center
until there's no whites only signs in children's minds

until there's no whites only signs in children's hearts
                         until the colored are free
                         until white people are free
                         until black people are free

                                             it keeps bleeding

we can't make it stop
or can we

                                             you can't make it stop
                                             or can you

do you turn away wallowing in guilt
delving deeper into a forgiveness
that doesn't exist
a forgiveness that ceased to exist
a forgiveness that will never exist
there's blood too much blood in South Africa and it's spilling over
there's blood too much blood in South Africa and it's spilling over
                         blood is spilling over on necklaces
                         blood is spilling over in Cité Soleil
                         blood is spilling over in garrisons
red is the color of the blood spilling over from makeshift boats in the Caribbean Sea
red is the color of the blood spilling over from makeshift boats in the Caribbean Sea
there's too much blood on this country I love
there's too much red on this country I love
                         this country that won't let children live
that kills them
in their mother's womb
so women now
give birth
to
stillborns
how do you keep yourself how do you keep yourself from wanting to touch from wanting to
smell from wanting to be from wanting to feel to find a peace that ceased to exist to find a peace
that never existed to find a peace that will never exist
to stop looking to stop looking for something
to stop looking to stop looking for anything
to stop looking to stop looking
so you can
find

if

if she had known when she first saw him that she would later lose her heart to him
she would have resisted she would have resisted the feeling that overtook her when
she was away from him she would have resisted the desperate need for water that
she suffered even though she had nearly drowned herself in the pint evian she refills
daily in the empty kelvinator   she wasn't concerned with her health anymore   she
was overcome with a need to have alcohol seep through her veins continuously
during the days so that she could exist as she did at night during sleep after she had
consumed a couple shots of rum with lime and sugar she had read in the new york
times magazine a true daquiri only contained fresh lime and sugar that became her
drink her source of salvation her solace especially when her mind would ignore her
and wander to him in places where it should not she not only became accustomed to
them she became dependent on them actually she began to depend on the feeling of
numbness it was more like a sense of deadness an inability to think or want or feel
or need that's what they did for her   they gave her that special feeling of numbness
that followed the gobbling of two true daquiris   one right after the other   of course
that always meant she had to have made them earlier left them in the fridge to
become cold she wouldn't dilute them with ice that's why they were in the fridge so
they could be cold like he told her she would become one day   if she had known
when she first saw him that she would lose her heart to him she would have resisted
she would have resisted the impulses that led her to him almost every day   he never
bid her to come nor did he ever call it wasn't his fault he didn't want to   he didn't
have to   he didn't have to besides she was always there   she was always already
there but in her heart she was responding to his summoning her she was responding
to a desire to have him summon her to have him bid her to come and see him
because he needed to see her if she knew she would lose her heart, her head and her
self when she first saw him she would have run away she would have run as far
away as her sandaled feet could take her in the two-o'clock-ninety-degree heat on the
dirt road that is mapped out in her head which intersects the street down from where
her heart resides she didn't know then but she knows now now she knows that's
why she's been having all these dreams that's why she's had this series of dreams
about her part in the polish resistance the dream about her making a deal with the
devil and abel and the other one about the frenchman and the watermelons

On Why the Hypocrite is the Righteous One, Or Words Misunderstood

I.
Last night he came over for dinner
i made the mistake of inviting him
trying to build a bridge i made a mistake
he spent the whole night regurgitating
the academic discourse that further alienates him as a brotha
but gives him nuff powers of domination over a sistah
one had to cry out that only english is spoken here
where we are
where we were
amongst ourselves with each other
a bunch of women who made the mistake
of inviting a man over to our house
when you invite a certain type of man to your house
you invite a ruler   an emperor—perhaps not
when you get the emperor in a reading
it represents a patriarchal structure of some kind
confrontation with authority a boss or father
someone who's not very easy to get along with
the emperor is not a bad card
No when you invite a certain type...
No i invited the son of swords
in his nakedness choking a dove
choking Aphrodite
choking himself
you're choking yourself man
X is detached from his heart
overly mental he is far from his sensitivity
he doesn't trust his intuitions
he dwells in possibilities but he never experiences
he wouldn't make love on the beach
too concerned with the tiny imprints left by grains of sand on his supple skin
which would find ways to hide in the crevices of the body
he was among us unaware that his voice rose above the decibels of ours
that his over four-syllable words that impress professors
white   black   convoluted professors
caughtupintheliminalspaceoftheoreticalanalysis
had no place with us
we know some of those words too
but we use them we use them when we have to
we were a bunch of women talking with ourselves
amongst ourselves about selves

we made—No i made the mistake of inviting a man who has never felt feelings rush up through his
veins to his heart his head from his loins leaving his mouth filled with saliva so much that he nearly
chokes because he can't he shouldn't spit it out until the feeling overwhelms him and he loses his
head

II.
Today
i had to call my grandmother at 4 p.m.
while i was still am here in Jamaica
it's 2:45 a.m. and i can't sleep
i'm writing this so-called poem
because   i can't   i won't rest until i do
until i let it pour itself out of me
filling these blue lined 69 cent yellow pages
with words that i will look back upon as judgmental
hypocritical and overly pretentious
Who the hell am i to judge when K touches me
god when he comes near me
my senses are immediately heightened
high on him
the vividness the redness
the vividness the fullness of his mouth
make me succumb to my passions
i become slave to...

                                        //can love exist without kisses//

i become slave
i become slave to the rhythm of his heart beats
i take his hand and close my eyes
and brush his palm onto my temple my ear my cheek my nose
my mouth my chin my cheek my cheek my ear
my temple my forehead my hair and
back again
until his hands have seen me like his eyes do
that's how i like to say hello to him
so that
his hands can see me like his eyes do
i like his hands
i like his whiteness against my skin
it's a crude reminder of what i am in the U.S. of A.
                of what he is in the U.S.A.
of what we are in the world   this first world
me-a-Black-Haitian-woman-a-Third-World-woman
what is the Third World?
His whiteness is a crude reminder of what we are on this planet
                        of what we are to each other
How can i want you as much as i do
you are my oppressor

my
d
o
w
n
p
r
e
s
s
o
r
i am a black woman
the black woman who wants to understand your pain
the black woman who wants to understand your love
                                                                    //can there be love without kisses//
the black woman who wants to understand your self
                                        your kisses
that leave me wanting to possess you
to make love with you for hours
for days
until we're both exhausted and grow—
(i wanted to write bored
but we could never be bored with each other
there's so much new)

Today i had to call my grandmother
because i got scared
something happened that i could not
did not understand
circumstances
too many circumstances
too many circumstances
that were connected led me to him
i got to the gallery
thoughts of Jean-Michel Basquiat invaded my mind
as i stepped into the room
onto which his soul was carved
I wanted it right away
i WANTED it
i wanted IT
enthralled i stood there
i just stood there unable to decipher
the different magnets that were pulling me in
the different magnets that were pulling me in
the different magnets that were pulling me in
deeper

into
the edge of
the blackness
                    the greenness
                              the redness
                                        the yellow of the words
                                                  the fishes
                                                            the words
            the heart of Ezili-Freda-Dahomey that
s
  l
    i
      d
        o
          f
            f
the canvas and coiled at my feet
                              i don't need professional help
                              i haven't loved him yet
that is if he ever lets me
i wasn't afraid of the snake
it wasn't really there
i knew i had to bend down pick it up and wrap it around my neck
i knew i had to bend down pick it up and wrap it around my neck
like the painting that i saw at the national gallery the night before
the snake is the mother
                    she is Earth
                              she is knowledge
                                        she is love
                                        she is pain
                                                  she is sex
                                                            she is pleasure
she is
she is Medusa
before she was distorted by men who are afraid of goddesses
she is the locked Medusa
before she was distorted by men
before she was distorted by men who are afraid
of strong women who know
what they need to
make themselves
come
she is love
                    she is life
                              she is power
Are you afraid of strong women
i would someday ask him

The snake
that snake
your snake is the one i worship
she is Dambala and Aida-Wedo
she hisses and brings terror
she hisses and brings terror
she hisses and brings terror into the hearts of those
those who don't know
those who don't know
how to express their passions
those who are afraid of surrender
those who are afraid of surrender
those who are afraid of surrender

i make love like that...
*inspired by Sandra Cisneros's "You Bring Out
the Mexican in Me"*

my knees folded beneath
my arms stretched above
giving
touching
feeling
always wanting to feel feelings beyond touch
i remember when i began to do this
i remember when i did this for the first time
it was with him
him
he was the man who would have validated my righteousness
my righteousness
righteousness that i later rejected
because hypocrisy always accompanies righteousness
it was with him that i began to make love like that

i make love like that
my knees folded beneath
my hands stretched above
needing
searching
looking
i keep my head down
no eye-to-eye contact
no!
no eye-to-eye contact
with my body i give him everything
everything my heart
that has not learned how to give
cannot give him
my heart
my independent heart
screams out for power over him
power over all men
power over him that i have when i keep my eyes down
let him think i exist for him
let him think i exist only for him and nothing else
i keep my eyes down he doesn't need to see the victory i know
he is at my mercy because i am on my knees
on my knees before him
he doesn't know

he doesn't need to know
i am powerful on my knees
i have been on my knees since i was born

i make love like that
my knees folded beneath
my arms stretched out above
submission?
no!
i was born like that in 1804
i was supposed to be free but i was forced to bow to
greater white powers that refused to respect my sovereignty
i was forced to bow to the creoles with their colonized minds
i was forced to bow to men and women like myself
who treated me cruelly as the whites who had brought me to this country
because in our eyes i was savage
after over 200 years i was still too african, too strong, too spiritual
not white enough, not nearly french enough
i make love like that because
i was born black in haïti
on my knees

i make love like that
my knees folded beneath me
my arms stretched above me
searching
feeling
always wanting to feel feelings that went beyond touch
i have been on my knees every night before going to sleep
merci seigneur pour cette journée que je viens de passer
fais que je passe une bonne nuit
sans danger sans malheur sans action et sans omission
bon dieu protège maman, papa, dona, amoutou
soeur élie même soeur cécil
with the tiny little wire rimmed glasses that rest on
her white red pudgy cheeks about to explode
forgive her for calling us *patat boukannen*
with our bony knees and flexible bodies
in blue/white checked uniforms
forgive her for she does not know that she has sinned
forgive her god for she does not know that she has sinned
i say this on my knees on concrete every night before sleep
these knees have been on concrete every night for eleven years
that's why i make love like that

i make love like that
my knees folded beneath
my arms stretched above

once i was on my knees for a whole night
on two books in the front room in the dark
bò kote chèz fè fòje yo
on kawo, on pik, on trèf, on kè
i remember mother coming to the room to see how i was
asking papa to let me, or was it dona, go to sleep in my bed
he said no i had to take my punishment
i don't even remember why i was being punished
i don't even remember why i had to spend the whole night on my knees
on two books in the living room while everyone else was asleep in bed
i remember praying
i prayed to god my real father
i imagined that i was the chosen one and j.c. was ponce pilate
but i wasn't going to be crucified like jesus
no!
i wasn't going to die on the cross
that's why i make love like that

i make love like that
my knees folded beneath
my arms stretched above
searching looking needing
because when god is too busy
i get on my knees and open my arms
and call papa legba to open the gates for me
so i can enter a place where i always feel safe
so i can enter a place where i am never forgotten
so i can enter a place where i am always protected
when i'm on my knees i'm with
ezili dantò, ezili freda, ogu feray, ogu badagri
tout les saints, tout les morts, tout les marassa
tout nasyon ginen
bò manman m, bò papa m
bò manman manman m, bò papa papa m
i am powerful on my knees because i am never alone
that's why i make love like that

i make love like that
my knees folded beneath
my arms stretched above
i keep my eyes down
no eye-to-eye contact so he doesn't see my victory
my hands searching touching feeling
always wanting to feel beyond touch
always wanting to feel beyond touch
always looking desperately needing searching
always desperately looking for home
that's why i make love like that

Parallels
My Country's in the Newspaper

Where you from? people ask
you see i look Jamaican—
rounded African features in a slightly oval frame
dark skin—i look like i'm at least from the islands
so why not Jamaica?
i'm here aren't i?
i could be...
i am Jamaican...
that is until i open my lips
and words give me away

Hey foreign! where you from [...] England?

a friend tells me that anyone who looks strange enough is considered English
i tend to get confused when anyone asks me that question
actually, i don't really get confused
no i get pissed
i get scared
because i'm being asked to define myself
to redefine myself
who i am
who i think i am
and   who i want to be

                                                                Where am i from?

                    Haïti.
that word never fails my mouth
it rests on the thickness in the air
that soon follows my response
Haïti?
you see i sound american
very american
and to a great degree i am
but down deep... down real deep
down real deep i know i am Haitian

Dem have a lotta AIDS over there she commented

i didn't respond i've gotten so accustomed to such responses
the other day Moses the taximan
got impassioned about what he called the stupidity of the Haitian people

That [the political situation in Haïti in the past decades] *could never happen*
in Jamaica he assured me
No, man Jamaicans are vile he boasted

That would never happen to Jamaicans
of course it wouldn't not militarily
it would have to be in disguise...
it would have to be a ruse
Jamaicans are being fucked too
unlike in my country they're being fucked silently less violently
                     black people are in a perpetual state of self hatred
                     black people are kept in a perpetual state of self hatred
                     black people are kept in a perpetual state of self hatred
          black people are being killed more slowly
out of many one—no color problem in Jamaica
Just class they say
in Jamaica there's no problem
i didn't let Moses in to hear these thoughts
i crushed them deep within deeper into my mind
afraid that these words were reactionary
that these words were merely words meant to lessen the pain, the hurt the weight that rises from
my chest presses up my throat disabling me from breathing like when my mouth fills up with
saliva in my nightmares and i can't scream for help i can't scream that i am terrified of
this feeling of helplessness
this feeling of distance
this feeling of forgetting and not wanting to forget
this feeling of not forgetting and wanting to forget
this feeling of being an immigrant
of being there and yet far away
of having this place that i call a country, this country my country
be a place that i only see on TV a place that i read about in newspapers

yesterday in the *Gleaner* i read about the military running rampage
in the countryside since the accord was signed on August 30th
they broke up a community meeting of Aristide supporters—killed a man
raped a twelve year old Girl

by the time i was twelve i was no longer in Haïti i was privileged
i had no consciousness about what it meant to be a young girl
what it meant to be a young black girl
from a country where we've been killing ourselves since 1804
by the time i was twelve i had just enough consciousness to naively vow
that i would never return to this country that i called my own
that i would never return until things "changed"
that i would never return until "things" changed
you see i made that decision after i first saw Haïti on TV
after i saw Haïti in the newspaper
i longed for answers...   answers to all the questions

at first, i used to say it was greed
that's why there was coup d'etat after coup d'etat
greed
then i would say it was our political-economic history
yes, we have a history of fucking over our own
since i've been in Jamaica i've been searching for other reasons
because the ones i claimed no longer suffice
when someone asked me for the non-academic version
i gave the same answer that i made myself believe for the last ten years
the same answer that explains this country (my country) that i see on TV
                              the country that i see in the newspapers
but you see i haven't been there in fifteen years i haven't seen
but you see i haven't been there in fifteen years i haven't seen
since i've been in Jamaica
i've come to see that my country's fucked up
for the same reason that a black Jamaican man can write a song
that echoes the voices of the majority of this population
a song about having no consciousness about who and what we are
a song about our lack of pride and blindness to the beauty in ourselves
a song about our fear of remaining black seeking only brown, yella, and white
because we've been taught to hate blackness to hate ourselves
a song about failed emancipation from mental slavery
how we're still very colonized

Out of many one—a disguise—a ruse
                              Where you from? they'll ask
                                        they'll ask again
the next time i'll just say
the same place as you

My Country In Translation

last sunday
i sat through a series of slides
one after another one after another
of haitian women children and men
in a hospital in limbé
slides one after another
one after the other
some of them i couldn't look at
without turning away
or covering my eyes
open gashes, tumors, abscesses
i heard a lot of medical terms
that i would forget in an hour
after i sat through the slides
one after another one after another

meanwhile
my mind travelled
to lansing to miami
back to the slides
and back again
to lansing and miami
to when i first began
to translate for the refugees

the first time i translated
i'd laugh
when i couldn't understand when i couldn't explain
when i couldn't find english words for this man's words
i couldn't find the words
because even in kreyòl or in french
they weren't part of my vocabulary
these words never were part of my vocabulary
because his life has never been mine
because the haïti i grew up in
the haïti i know didn't consist of these words
the haïti i knew didn't consist of these words

i continued to laugh
nervously
because i have never been to this haïti
but i was going back there
i was going back there with them

i was going back there with their words
as i translated
i   even   mimicked
pauses
hesitations
uneasy smiles
the quickness to say words
that once translated
would determine lives
WORDS determined young lives
i did that with all of them
in lansing and in miami

once while translating
my laughter got on the verge of
hysterics

when translating
i always asked them
if they understood me
then i would apologize
for not being able to translate properly
quickly enough
for not being familiar with some words
for not having understood everything
politely they'd say

kreyòl ou bon gina
pa gen pwoblèm se lang ou
ou pale kreyòl tankou ayisyen ou ayisyen

every time i think about lansing
about miami
i wonder if they know
i remember their words
i couldn't translate
those words i didn't know
i wonder if they know
these words give me
a little of the country i didn't know
i wonder if they know
these words give me
a little of the country that i used to know
a little of the country that i never knew

i Saw The Headlines Yesterday

walking... rushing down state street
letters leapt from the metal cases
i didn't want to stop
but my eyes lingered over each individual metal case
it was on the front page of at least three papers
it even made the front page of the *New York Times*

"Blacks' Killing Darkens South Africa's Dream"

i kept on my way, kept on walking
when i went to the café later
i avoided the papers again
until i had to go out last night i wasn't in a hurry then
my eyes leered over the cases catching every word
of every headline
slowly over each paper in each box
the yellow blue orange white one
what must be going through your mind
what must be going through your heart

today
i was back in the café i did read the paper
well... actually i wanted to read my horoscope
but i ended up reading the whole paper
and the *New York Times*
Chris Hani, head of the communist party
South Africa's most popular militant leader of the ANC
second only to Nelson

fears of angry blacklash could threaten talks on ending apartheid

*the South African government has actually acknowledged
that there was a conspiracy to carry out this terrorist act—
Hani's name was on a "hit list"—*

Hani wasn't killed because he was black, but because he was a communist leader

but it appears that the Polish immigrant in custody acted alone
right like Oswald acted alone
like James Earl Ray acted alone

                                subsequently, two white men were burned to death
                                        another had his tongue ripped out
                                i wish i could ask you how that makes you feel
                                        a white man from South Africa
                                i wish i could ask you how that makes you feel

                        does it scare you?

do you wish they could all disappear
or that someone could drop a special atom bomb on them
to get rid of them all
to just get rid of them
to get rid of them so you can find some peace
so you can dwell in a place
where horror no longer exists
a place in your whiteness
where you won't feel any guilt
so you can stop feeling
like there is something inside of you
that is eating away at your insides and it hurts
you can't get rid of it but, you just want it to stop
you just want it to stop
you just want it to stop
                        does it scare you?

that you want the horror to stop
but you can't make it stop or can you
                        does it scare you?

have you wished you were one of those men
burned to death
the one with his tongue ripped out
so he can never speak
not to saint peter
keeper of the gates to heaven
he can't even ask for forgiveness
for being a white man from South Africa
so he can never say that he is sorry
that there was nothing he could do
that he didn't know what to do
he didn't know how
                        does it scare you?

that you want the horror to stop
but you can't make it stop or can you

                                                    does it scare you?

do you wish you were one of these men
because even though your heart is bleeding
your skin is white
even though you may wish their pain their suffering could go away
your skin is white
even though you want to understand their anger
your skin is still white
in a country that is divided by color lines

but you can't make it stop or can you?
you can't make it stop or can you?
                                                    does it scare you?

could you sleep last night? did you sleep well? did you rise up and out of your body and float out
of your room, out of the house, outside? did you roam the streets? glide over the cars past the café,
to the arb? did you float through the trees in the arboretum? it's so quiet and so peaceful there.
oh look, right over there. yes there... aren't these flowers pretty. wait... be careful what's that?
there's something dripping from you.

A Poem About Why I Can't Wait,
going home again and again and again
Or:
Why I Prefer The Term Incarcerated When Talking About Agency

Gede Nibo gad sa vivan yo fè mwen
plante may'm mayi m tounen rozo
rozo tounen banbou
banbou tounen ponya
ponya yo ponyade m Gede

Every morning from the time I was three
I had to open my mouth to receive
two tablespoons full of emulsion scott
sometimes I would pinch my nose so I couldn't smell it
making it easier to swallow that pasty white liquid
that left my tongue tasting of salty tears and cod liver oil
often we had to chase it with homemade v-8
watercress, celery, beets, spinach, carrots and all sorts of
other things that grow in the earth to give little weaklings strength

Despite the grimaces   pouts   tears
despite the nos   the I don't want tos   the cries   the wails
the screams that often preceded this ritual eventually I would drink it
not because it's good for me
but because I had   I didn't have a choice
I had to open my mouth
let it slime down my throat
and swallow

When I was about fifteen
one day my father called all three of us into the living room
and told us we had to let go of our dreams and be serious about the future
poor man not even a son to carry on his name
he had been cursed with three girls
and we wanted to be a singer, a dancer and a writer
after calling us by our names he said
I want a doctor a lawyer and a dentist
I remember saying to him
I don't care if I never have any money
(though I would later change my mind)
I don't care if I never have any money

even if I live in a tent as long as I have my music
what are you asking me that I live this life my life for you?
In all my sassiness I dared him
and when would I live my life? when you die?
the horror on his face I have since forgotten
but I remember mother verbally mourning her wasted life
having given him her best years
and realizing that I only get to do this "life thing" once
so I was going to do this life thing on my terms
as long as I have a choice

I remember the first time I went back to Haïti
it had been seventeen years
but I had to hide in a hotel
so daddy dearest wouldn't know I was there
desperate to refill all the gaps in my past
I stole back memories at night to retrace my childhood
I begged my cousin to drive me around
to the house on Rue Darguin
but it was gone
replaced with an edifice that
breathed the same coldness as the pentagon
then we went to the gingerbread house
that too had been demolished and reconstructed
though the mango tree was still there
Le Petit Chaperon Rouge had been closed for years
vines interlaced with the iron of the gate

I went back again two years later
and I remember a conversation with a man
who has lived in Haïti longer than I did
this white man who says he loves my country
the country I saw in newspapers and on tv for seventeen years
the country that for the longest time I only went to in translation
we were talking about class and color I was asserting my Gramscian ideals
about the importance of and the need to fight both wars
the war of maneuver and the war of position
especially the war of position
so we can take back spaces
hence why I tie my head with a scarf when I go to those places
you think they care he replied they don't care about your aunt jemima head
uhmm even after over twenty years in this country
you still have no other references, I said quietly
oh these ethnic notions I thought enraged
after over twenty years in my country his social limits were intact
for me that was the end of the conversation after all this was not a teach-in

How do you overturn four hundred years of history in less than one century?

I've been thinking a lot about writing a poem
about the meaning of the word diplomacy
about how this word is just another four letter word
about how this word is just another way to say
I am going to fuck you
not only are you not going to enjoy it
but when I am done with you
you're sure to say thank you
and like my sistahgurl says
you might even pay me for it
in accrued debt interest

can life exist without ideals?
can life exist without dreams?
                            where does your soul go when all you do is function?
                            where does your spirit go when all you do is function?

I am only 31 and I am getting so cynical
I am trying not to be
I've been reading Shakti Gawain
trying to do creative visualization
trying to imagine

*<imagine all the people
living life in peace...>*

a better world so I can change my world
but I have been having a lot of difficulty
I keep remembering my friend B with her three kids
who after a year still can't get a job
its not because she's not qualified
or that she's not trying
but because she's not from the right family
she doesn't have the right connections
and her skin is too damned dark
worse
she doesn't play by the rules of the game
she doesn't do safe cocktail conversations
she was on the sidewalks in the 80s
bringing down the second revolution
she was there on the streets
in front of the palace
in front of ministries
in front of police stations
waiting
waiting to lay claim to dead bodies

no one else would acknowledge
for fear of losing their lives
you know in Haïti one often inherits social scars by association
you know in Haïti one often inherits fatal scars by association
scars
wars
social fatal
death by association
tell me how to imagine a better world in this place
tell me how to imagine a better world in this place
       where even after operation restore democracy
       that came bound with IMF loans
       International Mother Fucking loans for the structurally adjusted
where the rules of the game are:
I am going to fuck you
and you are not going to enjoy it
tell me how do you imagine a better world in this place
tell me how to imagine a better world in this place
where the rules of the game is this diplomacy
where blackness still equals poverty
where even after over 400 years
still too black too strong not french enough
never really french enough
and the new generations don't want to be man!

raging youths are now more committed
to seeing blood run
raging youths are now more committed
to seeing blood run
to seeing blood run on sidewalks
just to see blood run through the streets
next to expensive cars
outside of elite owned stores
because they say they have had enough
           jan'l pase, li pase
           jan'l mouri, li mouri
           however it goes down, it goes down
           however it dies, it dies
the end result is still the same
the revolution is not over

the revolution is not over they cry as they die
they have had too much adversity
this is the generational gap
don't need to ask them when are they going to grow up
           when are they going to grow out of this phase
           it is not a phase this is about the game

it was at the university that they learned the rules
through liberation theology they learned they were comrades
it was at the university that they learned
the multiple meanings of the word diplomacy
how you have to be pliable
acquiescent
don't make waves you don't get perks
no gains if you misbehave   a good little negre
that's what you are being trained to be
like the ancestor who sold my ancestor to the west
se depi nan Ginen nèg pa t vle wè nèg

Gede Nibo gad sa vivan yo fem mwen
plante mayi'm mayim tounen rozo
rozo tounen banbou
banbou tounen ponya
ponya yo ponyade m Gede

How do you overturn four hundred years of history in less than one century?

And I keep thinking back to my life here
and I keep thinking back to my life right here
in this white power center
aint no misbehavin' here
in the ivory tower
abounded white liberals and Marxist scholars
where liberalism is
rhetoric
defined as a floating signifier
associated with the ever growing ponytail
the peace sign
the old leather jacket from undergrad
the backwards baseball cap
the black power sign
nightly homage to the celestial herb to justify being a function
commitments
commitment to the metaphysics of diversity
commitments
commitment to the environment
to animal rights
the pet projects
and pet cultures
signifying signifiers are recreating structures
these signifying signifiers are recreating structures
these signifying signifiers are recreating bourgeois structures

bourgeois bourgeoisie bougi bouginess

blackness bouginess blackness
contradictions
disjunctures
                              underplayed identities
                              downpressing privilege
down
         down
down you got to keep it down
sometimes it just wants to rise up
but you gotta keep it down
SHUT YOUR MOUTH!
stuff it in your mouth
just keep your mouth shut and get out
ram it down your throat
deep down your throat
swallow
it
down
you're being forced
to deep throat
but I don't want to
I don't want to
swallow
         it
down
you gotta keep it down
you gotta keep it down
d
o
w
n
why you have to be down to keep it real
                              downplaying privilege
little white rebels wanna be niggers
and niggers wanna be   niggaz
bourgeois blues
opportunities denied
blackness bouginess
disjunctures?
contradictions?

In Haïti the bourgeoisie funded coups
in Jamaica uptown bougies tried to silence a revolution
but rastafari had a free black mind
so they self-fashioned an everyday resistance
the self-fashioning of everyday SEXIST resistance
                    an everyday HOMOPHOBIC resistance

they self-fashioned an everyday sexist and homophobic resistance

<don't let them fool ya
or even try to school ya>

blackness bouginess blackness
in the Caribbean bouginess has funded revolutions
little white rebels wanna be niggers
and rebelling niggers wanna be niggaz
these signifying signifiers are just recreating bourgeois structures

can life exist without ideals?
can life exists without dreams?
                    where does your soul go when all you do is function?
                    where does your spirit go when all you do is
function?

Lately, I have been thinking a lot about writing
a poem about class comfort
and color and privilege and guilt
about the social luxury of whiteness
about the social luxury of white skin
a poem about the rules of the game
and I think back to the keeping it real conference
how we had the rhetoric to deconstruct performance
the performance of blackness and black identities
but we couldn't talk about black privilege
for fear of having to talk about black guilt
like the good doctor says we can't talk
about the fact that we like trashing on the weak
because we don't have the courage
to confront the powerful
in this place
in this white power center
this bastion of liberalism
where anthropology incubates racism
where anthropology incubates racism
where anthropology incubates racism
this place of learning
who the players are
what the rules of the game are
and how to play and win
            how do you play knowing every moment in time your identity is in question?
            when do you win if at every moment in time your identity is in question?
I'm criminal
compulsive alertness
always having to be alert
criminal

always ready to answer questions
criminal
questions that never get asked
because of assumptions
that lead to even more questions

<what I need is a good defense
'cause I'm feelin' like a criminal>

How do you overturn four hundred years of history in less than one century?

Since this is about why I can't wait
I am gonna tell you why I am so tired
why I'm so tired
of not being able to imagine a better world
so I can change my world so we can change the world
why can't we talk about the things that make you wanna
can't talk about the things that make you wanna holler
make me wanna scream
cry
yell
let my people go
let my people go
right here
right now
right here
let me go
how far would we go
when we're still in chains
I can't wait
because I'm tired
tired of smiling
tired of masking
I'm tired of signifyin'
tired of being on the front line
tired of fighting the same damned
isms   daily
I am tired of wearing this suit of steel
I am tired of being weighed down by armor
I am tired of carrying a banner of love
while the war   still   rages

The Passion In Auto-Ethnography: Homage To Those Who Hollered Before Me

Silence chose me
I didn't choose silence
silence immobilized me
I could not breathe in my own skin
without breaking the silence
I could not live in the castle of my skin
as I came of age colonized
knowing I wasn't meant to survive I screamed
knowing the power of the erotics I screamed
using the erotics as power I screamed
out of my passion I screamed out
loud words that resonated the sound of a hammer going through flesh
screeches shrieks hollers screams
another woman hollering
hollers screams
another woman of color hollering
hollers shrieks
just another black woman hollering creeks
like caroline, catherine, ellen, ella
hollering shrieks
like zora, audre, gloria, sandra
hollering creeks that crack
hollering creeks to crack to shatter the screens that border the walls of the tower
that safeguards the gatekeepers mirrored crick-crack
krik!
krak!
cricks can crack the mirror
keep out the cricks that can turn into cracks
reaffirming their silences
the cricks in the crack
drowning our silences
hollering screaming silently suffocating
the cricks that make the crack
that be too wild and need to be tamed
the cricks that make the crack
that be too wild and need to be contained
the cricks in the crack that need to be erased
be that or disappear
fear or disappear
always disappear

crying hollering laughing they keep disappearing
because they love themselves they disappear
audre   barbara   flo
where are you?
they love themselves when they're laughing
I am just trying to love myself when I am crying
I'm just trying to love myself when I am hollering
challenging these disciplinary acts
trying to love ourselves when I try to take a stand
just trying to love myself when I stand tall
as ma sistahgurl jennifer says

Why do they think so many black women in anthropology keep turning to the arts?

using the erotic of power to redefine myself
I inserted myself in the diss
I inserted myself deep into the diss
I inserted myself into this form that stifles me
into this diss that reflects me
into this diss that can barely contain me
and from that point of knowing
I cried and screamed and hollered
                    about my blackness
I cried and screamed and hollered
                    about my baldness
the politics of being black
                    and the privilege of light skin
the politics of being bald
                    and obsessions with textured hair
the politics of coming of age colonized
                    and trying to define what it means to be free
the politics of recreating structured structures
                    and the denying of past spiritual agency
the politics of reaffirming silences
                    and the drowning out of loud voices
that   screamed   hollered   cried   laughed   before me
silently   loudly   hollering
objectivity has historically miseducated me
objectivity has historically suffocated me
through subjectivity I can be
only through reflexivity can I be who I am
not who you need me to be
through subjectivity I can take my oppression
I can name it and claim it
and try to resist remaining an occupied territory
because I wasn't just miseducated sister lauryn
my generation came of age colonized
comfort didn't choose me
I didn't choose comfort

I could not choose comfort
but I could not breathe in my own skin
so I tried to accommodate the angst
because i could not live in my own skin
I tried to get rid of the angst while suffocating
I and I hollered and screamed
I laughed to scream
screeches shrieks hollers screams
shrieking to crack
like those who came before me
because you and I know we have a date with history
I and I must know the time and place
so I can ask Papa Legba to open the gates for me
And in the name of all the saints all the dead all the twins
And the entire Ginen nation from my mother's side
And in the name of anacoana
And in the name of nanny of the maroons and nèg mawon
And in the name of cecile fatiman and soujourner truth
And in the name of jean jacques dessalines and toussaint louverture
And in the name of charlemagne peralte
And in the name of w. e. b. dubois and marcus garvey
And in the name of jean price mars and zora neale hurston
And in the name of angela davis and nikki giovanni
And in the name of patricia williams and peter tosh
And in the name of gloria anzaldua and maryse conde
And in the name of audre lorde and paulo friere
And in the name of winnie mandela and martin luther king jr
And in the name of irene diggs and roberta stoddart
And in the name of kathrine dunham and assata shakur
And in the name of malcolm X and mahatma gandhi
And in the name of shirley chisholm and michelle cliff
And in the name of ruth behar and michel rolph-trouillot
And in the name of faye harrison and nesha haniff
And in the name of walter rodney and bell hooks
And in the name of miriam makeba and elias farajaje jones
And in the name of betty lou valentine and john gwaltney
And in the name of lauryn hill and nelson mandela
And in the name of the sisters of the cowries
And in the name of june jordan and brenda cardenas and the last poets
And in the name of my mother my grandmother my great-grandmother
You and I have had a date with history
Eye and I need to know the time and place

IF NOT HERE, WHERE

IF NOT NOW, WHEN

Breathing Spaces

when I speak for myself
and say this place is stifling
and say this environment stifles me
and say this place was not meant for me
my voice often bounces back to me
framed by responses that further constrain me
in one too many of these instances i have choked
in one too many of these instances i have choked
i know I am not the only one here
so desperate for breathing space

I know i am not the only one here
so desperate for a different kind of space
a different kind of space where I can live in my own skin
a different kind of space where I can breathe in the castle of my skin

I know i am not the only one in search of breathing spaces
                                        different spaces
                                        different kinds of breathing spaces
I know i am not the only one
        desperate enough to keep harping on the need to lift the veils
        desperate enough to keep harping on the need to break silences
        desperate enough to stick my neck on the guillotine
knowing that
places like this don't answer
places like this don't forget
places like this don't forgive
especially new voices that become
the mirror
which forces
institutional
        memory
to
  r
    e
      s
        u
          r
            f
              a
                c
                  e
                    fragments

recreate
       f
      r
        a
         g
           m
             e
               n
                 t
                  s
demarcate
          fragments
fragmented voices that have been shouting
hollering
now become silent
        and then
new voices clash with the past
reviving fragments
recreating silences
that deny differences
that deny breathing spaces
         the elephant is in the room
         the elephant is in the room
         the elephant is in the room
silence only recreates silence
         the emperor has no clothes
         the emperor has no clothes
         the emperor has no clothes

hence why there is usually one
         a protector?

hence why there is always one
         a patron?

hence why there can be but one mistress here
no man
no woman will master me
hence why there can be but one mistress here
no man
no woman will play me
hence why there can be but one mistress here
where
all the women are white
all the blacks are men
and I have had to be brave
I have had to be brave

because
the elephant is in the room
the elephant is in the room
the elephant is in the room
t
h
e
e
l
e
p
h
a
n
t
i
s
i
n
t
h
e
r
o
o
m
and its presence serves us all

Circles Of Power Children Of Resistance, Or My Rules of Engagement

Sitting in the back of an air-conditioned tourist bus
snaking through the more presentable parts of old habana
I admit I have been an *enfant terrible*
a terrible terrible child
who unhappily absorbed rows of acid-rain-stained
colonial mansions with open jealousy windows
for protruding foreign eyes to stare
extended crossed legs reclined in hardbacked chairs facing
fifty's style tvs framed in wooden boxes with pointy legs
my foreign eyes protrude
desperate for a sense of the real cuba
not the folkloric performances
or well structured tours that
make a commodity of the revolution
and tied it to black insurrections of the past
while hiding away present-day black sufferrations

        global apartheid sister faye calls it
                shoutout to the Comaroffs

why is it that everywhere we go in the world
darker skinned people are always at the bottom
always at the end of the line?

I have been an *enfant terrible*
a terrible terrible child
arrogantly impatient
with the same circles of power
that came even with socialismo

I wanted to discover my cuba
get a sense of my cuba
not the guarded tours designed
to keep you away from the realities
silenced
because the revolution worked
        But it didn't fix everything
because the revolution worked
        But it didn't fix everything
because the revolution worked
        But it couldn't fix everything
        It could not fix everything

so now we pretend
that black blood flows through us
that we have black friends blackness is cuba
that cuba is a black woman with a big behind
with a fat cigar hangin' in her mouth

I wanted to find my cuba
not be force-fed black performances
of blackness made for tourist consumption
I have been a terror
so quick to question without
even giving it a chance to be
so quick to question without
even giving it a chance to be
                                        what ever it is
                                                whateva

I know I have seen it all before
I just came from haïti
it's the same thing wherever you go
black people at the bottom of the stairs
black people at the end of the line
black people in the back door
black people performing
recreating minstrelsy
five bucks for filming and picture taking please
blackness as commodity

            so what do you have to complain about now?
                                            she asked me

tired of my own repetitious tirades
about being force fed blacknesss
performances of blackness
folklore devoid of spirit
made to satisfy the urge to find roots
made to satisfy the urge to find roots
                                to claim roots where some exist
                                to claim roots where some exist
roots to justify diasporic existences
why the hell are we consuming here
stereotypical images we'd boycott over there

my spirit wanted to cry
                wail
                            scream
                                    holler

stop force feeding me blackness
stop force feeding me my blackness
stop fucking force feeding me my own blackness
I have been an *enfant terrible*
a terrible terrible child

Are you actually planning on staying in academia?
she asked me

there are rules you know
you have to play by the rules
until you can get to a point
where you will have power
and eventually make changes
and make your own history

MAKE my own history
Make my OWN history
Make my own HISTORY

my history has already been made
do I have to name them
retrace the lineage
my lineage
your lineage
Our lineage

the millions and millions of lives
of pacifists
of fighters
of warriors
the lives of those
who committed suicide
who fought
who claimed freedom and made it theirs
who died
why do I have to start over
why do I have to start over
why do I have to start over
and recreate the wheel that they were tied to
and recreate the wheel that they had to go through
and recreate the training wheel   lab rats
wheels that keep going and going and going
and going and won't stop
until we say we won't get on the bus
because the road has been mapped
the road has been traveled before

the rails of this road had been forged
by the billions and billions of feet
footsteps of those who
bled and died
so we could stand here
so I can stand here
facing you
                              impatiently waiting
to hear you tell me when I can move
to hear you tell me when I can take
                              the step that won't offend
                              the step that won't threaten
                              you

when knives and daggers surround me
I don't fight
I get on my knees and I pray
I scream
when my spirit is under siege
I don't fight
I holler while waiting for deliverance
waiting for deliverance
that won't come
for a deliverance
that can't come
because the wheel spins and spins and spins
only to keep spinning and won't stop
until we say we won't get on the bus
this is why I can't wait
no this is why I won't wait
too many have died for me to be here
too many have already died for me to stand here
waiting
                  waiting
wondering when you will face me and finally admit
that this is not a duel
you didn't bring your weapons
hell! you've hidden your weapons
so we can't fight

so I have to decide
I have to decide
I have to recreate the wheel
if I get on this training wheel
my spirit will weaken
my spirit will weaken
in this cage that is yours
my spirit will weaken in this cage

that is your stage your fortress
your power your ivory tower
this is why I can't wait
this is why I must   rage
this is why I yell and will always holler
silence is suffocating me
and if I don't speak
and if I decide to play by the rules
will I know me
will I remember me
who I am and who I am supposed to be
pacifist?
fighter?
warrior
self-protector
who will guide me
who will lead me if I abandon my soul
I have been an *enfant terrible*
a terrible terrible child

When my spirit is under siege
I look to the future and feel weak
I look to the future and feel weak
knowing that knives and daggers surround me
while I wait for history to absolve me
while I wait to make a history
knives and daggers surround me
waiting for me to make a move
waiting for me to try to whisper cricks
not cracks
cricks cracks
crick crack
krik
–krak
shrieks to fill silenced spaces
once full of loud voices
that have been drowned by the circles of power
threatened by terrible children tied to their truths
terrible terrible children bound to their truths
unruly narrow-minded children
who need a long time

to accept that they come from
long lines of
pacifists
fighters

warriors
who have already paid their dues
they have already paid my dues
so when I tell you I won't start here
because my ancestors have already been there
so when I tell you I won't start here
because my ancestors have already been there
know that I am on the offense
know that I have declared war
know that I shall win
since I am here for but one reason
I am here to face you
I am here to look you in the eye
and challenge you to duel
I am here to claim back my spirit
        while standing on the piles of dust
        made of the carcasses of my ancestors
to take it and let it be
let it roam the streets of this earth while looking above
searching for a higher self
because my dear enemy
my dear friend
after all   that   is really
all I was brought
down here to do

Ode To The Metrès
Going Home: On Learning How To Glide

Nwaye m ape nwaye
Nwaye m ape nwaye

Ezili si ou wè m tonbe lan dlo pran m non
Metrès si ou wè m tonbe lan dlo pran m non
sove lave zanfan yo nwaye y ape nwaye

Nwaye m ape nwaye
Nwaye m ape nwaye

Ezili si ou wè m tonbe lan dlo pran m non
Metrès si ou wè m tonbe lan dlo pran m non
sove lave zanfan yo nwaye y ape nwaye

Nwaye m ape nwaye
Nwaye m ape nwaye

Ezili si ou wè m tonbe lan dlo pran m non
Metrès si ou wè m tonbe lan dlo pran m non
sove lave zanfan yo nwaye y ape nwaye

I was back home
when I saw you just standing there
you must have seen me too
you came to me you told me you loved me
that night I swam towards you
and told you I'm falling in love with you
I don't like this term falling you said
I mean I really don't like this analogy of falling
it suggests such a fateful end
when you fall you end up crashing
crashing on the ground
all the way into the ground and then you drown

no no no   I said,
in my   mind   I thought there is never any drowning
for the Metrès is always there
there is no crash
there is never a crash
you do fall and you fall and you keep falling
when it looks like there is nowhere else to go
you fall deeper and deeper into the fall
you fall and keep falling into ad infinitum
until the universe embraces you
and propels you to glide

Nwaye m ape nwaye
Nwaye m ape nwaye

Ezili si ou wè m tonbe lan dlo pran m non
Metrès si ou wè m tonbe lan dlo pran m non
sove lavi zanfan yo nwaye y ape nwaye

Nwaye m ape nwaye
Nwaye m ape nwaye

Ezili si ou wè m tonbe lan dlo pran m non
Metrès si ou wè m tonbe lan dlo pran m non
sove lavi zanfan yo nwaye y ape nwaye

Nwaye m ape nwaye
Nwaye m ape nwaye

Ezili si ou wè m tonbe lan dlo pran m non
Metrès si ou wè m tonbe lan dlo pran m non
sove lavi zanfan yo nwaye y ape nwaye

Basquiat's Lwas

The spirits in Jean-Michel Basquiat's head agitated
with all their puissance, they tormented him
until they did his body in

they made their first appearance in abrupt spurts of squiggly
black   lines   that   ate   through the whiteness of canvasses
to announce their claim on him

lwas get jealous when nonbelievers with inherited
duties disrespect the order of things and pretend
the price for such denial is high
spirits always find ways to their rapture

so they obsessed him until he gave them form
in iconic signs block letters
crowns
flies
crosses
snakes
numbers
griots
still they took over eating his flesh from within

no one had bothered to tell Jean-Michel
that his spirits needed to be nourished
can't feed one demon and starve the others

when his *mèt tèt* finally came out in full without regalia
nude   all in black   no cane   not even the   top hat
teeth bared   fearful and randy   he was already the winner

years after his body passed
                              under water
                                        on the way back to Ginen
the silence continues
                    as if no one could tell

Papa Gede danced in Jean-Michel Basquiat's head

Rodin's Kiss

twisted
bodies
intertwined
struggle
without
interfering
with the
union
of the
sexes

I
came
of
age
colonized
then
Rodin's Kiss
became

Dambala&Aidawedo

New Rules of Engagement: A Remix

You and i have had a date with history been standing here facing you for some time now impatiently waiting to hear you tell me when i can move **I can't breathe** to hear you tell me when i can take the step that won't offend the step that won't threaten you **I can't breathe** in one too many of these instances i have choked always a *bête noire* refusing to wait for a deliverance that won't come a deliverance that can't come **I can't breathe** as the wheel spins and spins and spins **I can't breathe** only to keep spinning and won't stop until we say we won't get on the bus and actually don't get on the bus **I can't breathe** too desperate for spaces where i can live in my own skin where we can breathe in the castles of our skins **I can't breathe** this is why i can't wait this stops today eric garner said this is why we can't we won't wait too many have already died continue to die for us to be here **I can't breathe** as spirits are under siege and bullets fly we keep waiting for history to absolve us **I can't breathe** so when i tell you i won't start here because my ancestors have already been there **I can't breathe** when we say we won't… can't start here because our ancestors have already been there you better know that we are on the offense **I can't breathe I can't breathe** in this battlefield spinning new manifestos for dreamers while standing on the bodies of our young and the carcasses of our ancestors ready… **to breathe**

A Manifesto for Dreamers

For Robin D. G. Kelley,
Freedom Dreams: The Black Radical Imagination

When Goya's Saturn picked up his son
and devoured him head first
He wanted to keep him from dreaming

When Goya's Saturn picked up his son
and devoured him head first
He wanted to keep him from dreaming

When Goya's Saturn picked up his son
and devoured him head first
He wanted to keep him from dreaming

An Alter(ed)native in Something Other than Fiction

'VooDooDoll'
What if Haïti
were a Woman: On ti Travay sou 21 Pwen

(1) **The Doll:** She is no longer as plush in certain areas as she once was in her days of glory. Still from afar, she resembles a human cake adorned with what could be candied poles with flowing streamers ready to be served at the next supper. Further inspection shows these to be tattered flags bearing national emblems & family crests. More scrutiny reveals the poles as pins pricked so close to parts of her that an estimate they cover nearly 80% of her surface would not be an exaggeration.

Each needle that now protrudes from her is well wedged into the hypodermis. They had either been carefully placed in various points away from her meridians to provoke nervous conditions or were thrown par hazard from some distance. Flying arrows from blindfolded archers seeking to impress their rivals. Those who made their mark got 10 points. The ones who did not received 30. There is always a reward. The game was not about winning but an exercise in devotion to the sport. It is always the dare.

(4) The Numbers: The ones that really matter actually remain unknown. Quantitative analysis may anchor some studies they have done little to disrupt entrenched beliefs that fermented long before she became synonymous with backwardness & evil. What we still don't know is the number of religious missions offering her food, clothing, shelter, education and of course salvation. Or the actual number of offsprings young and old whose laden J distorted perejil to their fatal detriment. The contested estimates range from 20,000 to 35,000 depending on which side of the border you ask. We know the initial value ascribed to the collective lives of the dead $750,000 would later be reduced to $525,000. 5+2+5=12. 1+2=3. Triad. A triumvirate or just another Holy Trinity. That is between $17.50 and $26.50pd (per dead). In actuality, the payment received was a personal draft for $250,000 and $25,000 in palm oil. And that would be between $7.14 and $12.50 pd (per dead). We don't know whom if any among the massacred actually benefited from this transaction. But we do know that she has long been a site for the trading of human chattel. In fact, years after she claimed her freedom, one of her sons agreed to an indemnity payment of ₣150,000,000 to her former master for recognition and respect that never really came. What we know for certain is that loaded term with its 4 dangerous little Os was cross-stitched within the folds of her skin to continuously distort perceptions of her. In quotation on Google, it results in 27,300,000 hits in 13 seconds. The one that ends in "ou" yields 3,870,000 in .28 while The one with "oux" produces 13,600 hits in about 6 seconds. And the original "Vodun" 120,000 hits in .26 seconds. All of that, of course, was well before 1/12/2010.

(7) The Rage: It is as if her rage has been suppressed or at the very least continues to be evenly and properly guarded. Managed. Gagged and bound with both arms seeming loose. Wrists crossed behind her. Ankles one on top of the other. Christ-like, angled downwards disciplined by the sheer weight of pieces of broken chain held together with wet silken ropes. No one talks of who actually tends to these. The wet ropes. Though we know they continue to gain strength with more moisture…. Molasses. Honey. PalmOil. Toes strained. En pointe. Seeking contact with the earth. How did she get here? A slight move, a purposeless shove or a well directed intended push from a passerby certainly guarantees her rotation. Why she is still here obsesses those who refuse to grasp that alone, she could not have hooked herself so above ground. She remains perched high on this extended branch constantly twirling for all to see her once revered beauty. No one wants to hear her. Very few will pay attention to her screams. When sounds escape her lips especially in mixed company, almost without fail, someone in the audience will recall the presence of white saviors.

(9) Her Silence: And if her rage remains unspoken, unexpressed, then what becomes of it? One too many have pontificated on the enigmatic mad white woman relegated to the attic. She who dared to question social mores that incarcerated her or turned her into the wallpaper. Less is known of this black female rage. There is usually no place for it. Its very articulation regardless of how much politesse is another social death sentence or better punishment for those uncontrollable REMEMORIES bound to stay crushed in her body, her archive. She dares not speak. Shut your mouth. Shhhhhhh…. Careful. There is no place for unruly girls like you who do not know when to be quiet. Shhhhhhhhhhhhhh… When to not offend white sensibilities. When not to choke. Swallow. When to submit. Shhhhhhhhhhhhhhhhhhhhh—Take a deep breath. Swallow… Swallow… Swallow…There is no safe word.

(11) The Experts: It is exhausting to hear this he exclaimed. And it is as exhausting to live it, she mused though she did not utter a single word. Thank you so so much for your performance in this academic setting offered the gatekeeper in response. Translation=the visceral has no place here. Keep it at home or on the stage. As if we are not all performers. She was too accustomed to such backlash. He was the first to speak. Inarticulate guilt without any restraint. A staccato of shame. A white German man he stands facing her and hands her a small piece of flat white carton with his name carefully embossed in his language.

D-i-s-s-o-c-i-a-t-i-o-n.

She imagined him The White King of La Gonâve. I know more of your history than you will ever want to know she muttered with the beginning of a welcoming smile that had him lean forward just so to await her assault. She flicks the lit wick then composes her thoughts. Compression. The conversations inadvertently turned towards those who have come with goodwill. To make changes. To give to the needy. I can save you. No one even whispers about what they reject. No one hears those who dare to shout about what they know. Sir, you need to speak either English or French only two people in this room speak Kreyòl. Rather coarse exclusionary practices. By the power invested in me, I assure you that I & I alone can fix you. Even more mumbo jumbo.

Not wanting to play nice, she does an improper curtsy to refute the rules. Why? Why should she? Why should she tell? Why should she fucking tell? Why should she fucking tell????? This bloody academic spectacle... depends on their endless fascination with zombies.

(14) The Debt: All but 21 of the trillion pores ooze nursed envy. If with interest 90,000,000 gold francs reduced from the original 150,000,000 gold francs is equivalent to

21,
685,
235,
571.
48
in 2004.

Then what would be her value in
cowries
today?

Desperate for recognition, she borrowed.
Of course, they lent.

(16) The Blame: The orchestra began before maestro took to the podium. With his usual swagger, he retrieved himself from the wall. Top hat cocked just a little to the left. Cane flipped balancing on forefinger. "Géde men lajen" the string section began. No 1 made his pledge. Leopold could not attend so he sent in a proxy. DM. One tugged at a wrist. Canada. Another pressed one ankle. 3. They were playing drowning by numbers again. $$$$ Throwing Gilders into a bucket full of blood drained when she was last prone. Must miss mark. Another grabbed an elbow. Never the voyeur, he marveled at the debacle at this round table. €€€€ . Monitoring her will, no 7 whispered loud enough for the friendly bidders to hear: "Don't get uppity with me my little negresse you are still my slave." Savoring the delights in the obscenity of being done, she reminded them Bismark had left instructions of proper carving techniques. Never too deep or far apart. "Gédé men lajen" the brass was way off key. No 8 tried to impress his rivals to earn more favors. Then the debate started. Was it 316, 000 or 60,000??????? Regardless divided into $5,000,000,000=$15,822pd or $83,333,333pd No one had yet said aloud what they were already thinking: "You're a little too greedy my pet even the gods would cry foul." The chorus started chanting in falsetto. Faster than a teenage vampire, he jumped onto the table. With his slowest gyration on record to date, maestro bellowed, Apa nou youn pa kon konté before breaking into laughter. A forgiving riposte for those who took his name in vain. They forgot to add the 6,000 lest we forget the 500,000 in waiting. More laughter before humming "Don't drink the water" FFF When the daredevil reached for her hem, he did a rassemblement. Cane turned into épée lodged gingerly on collarbone in that cave at the base of her throat. How could you do that to her? They all demanded. In concert. Even the hypocrites who thought she could stand to lose a few. The frequency of what emerged from his throat shattered through Slash's riff: "Petty little mortals, all you know how to do is RECREATE."

I Am A Storm

Tranble

tranble tè a tranble
tranble tè a tranble

Ezili si nou tranble ankò
pran nou
Metrès si nou tranble ankò
pran nou
sove pitit lakay yo
tranble tè a tranble

trembling the earth trembled
trembling we are trembling

Ezili, should we tremble again
hold us
Metrès, should we tremble again
hold us
save the lives of your children
tremble the earth is trembling

Skin Castles
for George Lamming

I. Contact
In the castle of my skin,
I
In the castle of my skin,
I
In the castle of my skin,
I
Look!
Look!!
Look!!!
A Negro…
On that island, the offspring of a white man and a black woman is a mulatto; the
mulatto and the black produce a samba; from the mulatto and the white comes the
quadroon; from the quadroon and white comes the mustee; the child of a mustee
by a white man is called a musteffino; while the children of a musteffino are free by
law and rank as white persons, for all intent and purposes.

And further up north, there was the one-drop rule. All—it—took—was—
one—d-r-o-p.

II. Bleeding
Mwen di Feray'o m'blese.   (Feray I am wounded)
Feray'o m'blese.   (Feray I am wounded)
Gade'm blese Feray.   (Look I'm wounded)
Mwen pa wè san mwen.   (I don't see my blood)
Mwen di Feray'o m'blese.
Feray'o m'blese.
Gade'm blese Feray.
Mwen pa we san mwen
In the castle of my--

III. Dying
Saint Philomene vierge martyre
Accorde nous misérecorde
Saint Philomene vierge martyre

Saint Philomene vierge martyre
Accorde nous misérecorde
Saint Philomene vierge martyre

The strong black woman is dead

The strong black woman is dead
The strong black woman is dead

Her silence killed her last night

Saint Philomene vierge martyre
Accorde nous misérecorde
Saint Philomene vierge martyre

In the castle of my skin

IV. Being

She never ever apologized for who she was.   With her there was no pretense. There was no shame. What you saw was what you got. She was a peasant, **so what**. She was illiterate, **so what.** She was a street vendor, **so what**. She had a lot of children, **so what**. She smoked a pipe, chewed tobacco and was a heavy drinker, **so what**. She was a Vodouist who loved to serve her spirits, **so f-u-c-k-i-n-g what**.

Athena's Rant on Good & Bad Neighbors

Imagine that you are living your life in a trailer, an apartment, a house in the suburbs with a white picket fence, or a mansion. Now imagine that the neighbor next door in the other trailer, duplex or the penthouse or up the road in the bigger suburban house or MTV crib decides to come around your yard and tell you how to run your affairs.

Imagine that forty years ago when your parents were alive in the same place, these neighbors didn't even talk to them because your ancestors had showed them up. They stepped out of line. But once these neighbors needed your parents, they started to talk to them even though in their eyes, they would never be good enough.

Imagine that they started to meddle in your household. They have all sorts of advice, because they believe they are better than you. They know what is best for you, which is not surprising as it always serves their interests. Everyone else tells them so, including your own family members who are rightly fearful of what life would be like without their protection.

Imagine that their concern, they say, is because you share the same street corner. You don't always agree but you need them. They built your roads, they put in electricity and they buy from your garden. They have the power to influence all of your other customers into boycotting your products.

How do you deal with them when they cross the line? Do you feel dissed? Should you, would you, could you… do anything?

If you ask me, not enough has been written about the respect and politeness of a nation that has been invaded and penetrated by its biggest and baddest neighbor. Haïti, like other nations in the hemisphere, is just another small square on a global monopoly board. Indeed, no one has talked enough about all of the disrespect Haïti has endured over the years by the most powerful nations in the world (especially France, the U.S. and yes, even Canada).

1849-	1851-	1857-	1858-	1865-
1866-	1867-	1868-	1869-	1876-
1888-	1891-	1892-	1902-	1903-
1904-	1905-	1906-	1907-	1908-
1909-	1911-	1912-	1913-	1915-

During every single year mentioned here, United States navy fleets either surrounded Haïti or threatened to come onto the island shores in order to "protect" their interests. They finally did come onto the island. In 1915, they landed on the shores and stayed until 1934. They came back again in 1994–1996 to offer much needed deliverance and then again for our bicentennial in 2004. All these years don't even include the times that secret ops of all kinds were going on in the country. Word is that they are not too different from the ways they do it in those spy movies.

Now let's imagine again that the bully of a neighbor of yours, no no no, not the one next door who farmed bones at the end of their massacre river, the other one.

Imagine they came sniffing around your pad nearly thirty times and with each visit got increasingly aggressive. He insists that he is watching out for your well-being. You feel scared. Threatened. Under siege. You get increasingly worried. You make friends because you hope that will work. Not all of you agree this is the best solution.

Others attempt to file a police report to no avail because the neighbor has not threatened to physically harm you and is smart enough to couch each trespass in terms of your common wellbeing. You can't get a restraining order, but you know that you are being stalked. So what can you do? Get a bodyguard? Go to the UN? Do you hire mercenaries?

Until 2001, in the U.S., the concept of being vulnerable was especially difficult for most rich people born after the Second World War to grasp. That changed to some degree with 9/11. Now imagine living in a country where the idea that others can come in at will is not strange but an expected occurrence, as we have lived with it for so long.

Perhaps, those of us overly fascinated with respect are that way because we, as a nation, never quite received it from most of the world. In fact, we have always had to fight for it. In Haïti, we have been living with terror alerts of one kind or another since before the day we were born.

I Am A Storm

showers of teardrops
are falling
they carry memories
of the beginning
when shadows of the wind
wrap the sky with its clouds
when the aged innocence
released her anger
she declared me a storm

I am a storm
I am a storm

I am thunder
I am lightning
I'm the grey
I'm the grey

I am thunder
I am lightning
I am the one you will call
when the guards are changing

there's no beginning
without ending
you are the one they call
the world needed changing
shadows of the wind
wrapped the sky with your clouds
and the aged innocence
released her anger
and made you into a storm

You're a storm
You're a storm

You are thunder
You are lightning
You are grey
You are grey

You've been thunder
You've been lightning
You're the one they call
World needed changing

no new beginnings
without ending
you are the ones we'll call
when the guards need changing
when shadows of the wind will
wrap the sky with its clouds
and the aged innocence
released her anger
and declared you a storm

I am a storm
You're a storm

We are thunder
We are lightning
We're the grey
We're the grey

We are thunder
We are lightning
We're the ones that they call
when the world needs changing

For
Dirette Perchotte and the Marassa

Credits

p. 11 *A woman who had become barren…* Joshua Trachtenberg. 2004 [1939]. *Jewish Magic and Superstition: A Study in folk Religion*. Philadelphia: University of Pennsylvania Press.

p. 66 *Imagine all the people…* John Lennon, "Imagine," 1971.

p. 70 *Don't let them fool ya…* Bob Marley, "Could You Be Loved," 1980.

p. 71 *What I need is a good defense…* Fiona Apple, "Criminal," 1996.

p. 106 *Look!…* Frantz Fanon. 1967 [1952]. *Black Skin, White Masks*. New York: Grove Press.

p. 106 *On that island…* Fernando Henriques. 1958 [1953]. *Family and Colour in Jamaica*. London: MacGibbon & Kee.

Versions of some of these poems and performance texts have been published in the following publications: *e-misférica, Gastronomica, Liminalities, MaComere, Meridians* and *Transitions*.

"Basquiat's Lwas" first appeared in *An Anthology of Haitian Women's Poetry*, edited by Claudine Michel, Multi-cultural Women's Presence, 2005; and was reprinted in *In Extremis: Death and Life in 21ˢᵗ Century Haitian Art*, exhibition catalogue, edited by Donald J. Cosentino, Fowler Museum at UCLA, 2012.

Excerpts from "Because When God is Too Busy" are published in *Let Spirit Speak! Cultural Journey Through the African Diaspora*, edited by Vanessa K. Valdes, State University of New York Press, 2012.

Excerpts from "Because When God is Too Busy" are recorded on Gina Athena Ulysse's CD *I Am A Storm* to benefit Inured.org. Produced at Kamoken Studio, Brooklyn NY, 2010.

Excerpts from "Because When God is Too Busy" are published in *Brassage: An Anthology of Haitian Women's Poetry*, edited by Claudine Michel, Multi-cultural Women's Presence, 2005.

"My Country in Translation" first appeared in *Resisting Racism and Xenophobia: Global Perspectives on Race, Gender, and Human Rights*, edited by Faye V. Harrison, AltaMira Press, 2005.

"Concepts of Home" was reprinted in *Women on the Verge of Home*, edited by Bilinda Straight, State University of New York Press, 2005.

"A Poem About Why I Can't Wait" first appeared in *The Butterfly's Way: Voices from the Haitian Dyaspora in the United States*, edited by Edwidge Danticat, Soho Press, 2001.

Author photo: Lucy Guiliano

Acknowledgments

The prolonged process that brought this book into the world simply includes too many mortals to be named here.

From the heart, I extend profound gratitude to: those whose artistry and critical inquiry stir me; those whose works have inspired me towards the remix; those who invited me to present this work, gave feedback and genuine critique; those who continue to be generous with their support and those I encountered on this journey seeking the foundation of my being. Sincere thanks for being a constellation of blessings.

Una Osato, William Electric Black at LaMaMa and Charles Knight (HIP) certainly deserve honored mention. At Wesleyan University Press, I appreciate Suzanna Tamminen's undeterred foresight; and Victoria Stahl, champion of my artistic endeavors, had a vision. I am grateful to the anonymous reviewer who helped me discard a chunk of the past to reframe the project.

Finally, my deepest respect and recognition goes to the dead, the ancestors and the family spirits. *Nou konnen*, I bow only in *your* presence.

About the Author

Gina Athena Ulysse is a feminist artist-academic-activist, or self-described post-Zora interventionist, originally from Pétion-Ville, Haïti. Her creative works include spokenword, performance art and installation pieces. Her poetry has appeared in several journals and collections. She is the author of *Downtown Ladies: Informal Commercial Importers, a Haitian Anthropologist and Self-Making in Jamaica* and *Why Haiti Needs New Narratives: A Post-Quake Chronicle*, and is professor of Anthropology at Wesleyan University in Middletown Connecticut.